SCIENCE WORKS

STAYING ALIVE

THE STORY OF A FOOD CHAIN

IT'S SIMPLY MOUTH-WATERING!

Jacqui Bailey Matthew Lilly

Picture Window Books • Minneapolis, Minnesota

Editor: Jacqueline A. Wolfe
Page Production: Melissa Kes
Creative Director: Keith Griffin
Editorial Director: Carol Jones

First American edition published in 2006 by
Picture Window Books
5115 Excelsior Boulevard
Suite 232
Minneapolis, MN 55416
1-877-845-8392
www.picturewindowbooks.com

First published in Great Britain by
A & C Black Publishers Limited
37 Soho Square, London W1D 3QZ
Copyright © Two's Company 2003

Printed in the United States of America.

Library of Congress Cataloging-in-Publication Data
Bailey, Jacqui.
Staying alive : the story of a food chain / by Jacqui Bailey ; illustrated by Matthew Lilly.
p. cm. — (Science works)
Includes bibliographical references and index.
ISBN-13: 978-1-4048-1595-7 (hardcover)
ISBN-10: 1-4048-1595-3 (hardcover)
ISBN-13: 978-1-4048-1998-6 (paperback)
ISBN-10: 1-4048-1998-3 (paperback)
1. Food chains (Ecology)—Juvenile literature. I. Lilly, Matthew, ill. II. Title.

QH541.14.B34 2006
577'.16—dc22   2005032669

For Chris
JB

For David and Elizabeth
ML

Special thanks to our advisers for their
expertise, research, and advice:

Larry M. Browning, Ph.D., Professor
Physics Department, South Dakota State University
Brookings, South Dakota, USA

Dr. Robin Armstrong, Peter Tandy,
and Charlotte Stockley
Mineralogy Department
Natural History Museum
London, England

Susan Kesselring, M.A.
Literacy Educator
Rosemount-Apple Valley-Eagan
(Minnesota) School District

3

One Food Chain's Story

It was the middle of the day in the African savanna, and the sun's heat baked the land like an oven.

Sunlight sparkled on the surface of a small lake. Every now and then, the snout of a hippopotamus bobbed up and down in the water.

Savanna is the name given to the hot, tropical grasslands found in parts of Africa, Asia, Australia, and South America. Different types of savanna have different animals and plants living in them.

A short distance from the lake, a tree stood among the grasses and shrubs. The sun blazed down on the tree.

The tree needed the sunlight. Without it, the tree could not grow and make its food—and without food the tree would die.

5

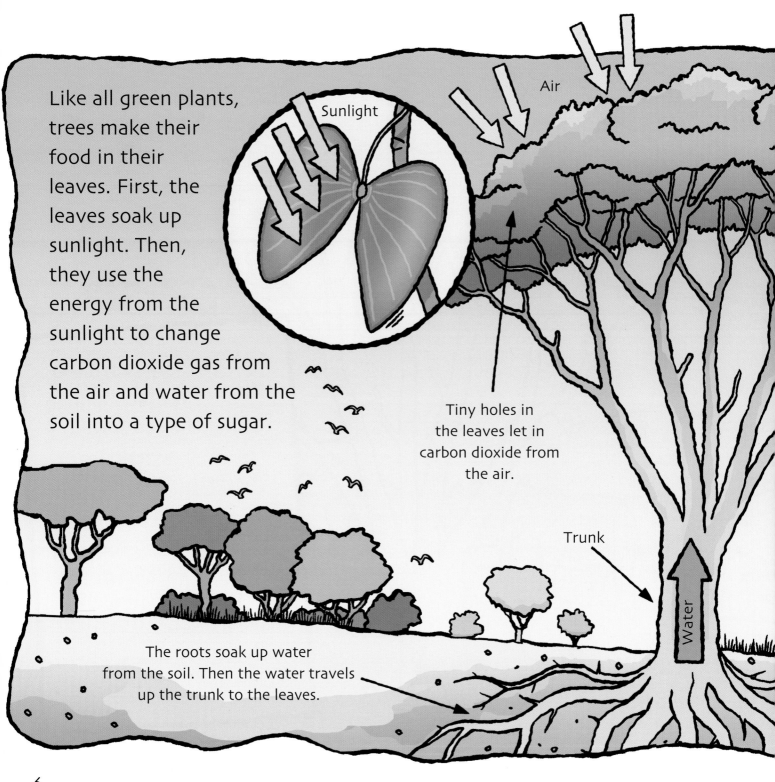

Like all green plants, trees make their food in their leaves. First, the leaves soak up sunlight. Then, they use the energy from the sunlight to change carbon dioxide gas from the air and water from the soil into a type of sugar.

Sunlight

Air

Tiny holes in the leaves let in carbon dioxide from the air.

Trunk

Water

The roots soak up water from the soil. Then the water travels up the trunk to the leaves.

I'M A FOOD FACTORY.

SLURP!

SLURP!

The sugary food that trees make gives them energy to grow and to make more leaves, as well as fruit and seeds. They also store some of the food inside their trunk.

The tree needs water, air, and sunshine to grow. To be strong and healthy, the tree also needs tiny bits of chemicals called minerals. The minerals are in the soil and the trees suck them up with the water through their roots.

Plants are living things, and all living things need energy to stay alive. Humans and other animals get their energy by eating food, but trees and other green plants make their food inside themselves. The way that plants make food is called photosynthesis (foe-toe-sin-theh-sis).

In the dry season, when the savanna had very little rain, the soil dried up. The tree and the other plants had no water. They struggled to make food and to stay alive.

I'M SO THIRSTY!

The African savanna is hot all year round. It does not have hot summers and cold winters. Instead, it has dry seasons when almost no rain falls, followed by wet or rainy seasons when a lot of rain falls.

The leaves on the tree turned brown and fell to the ground. The tree had to live on the food stored in its trunk.

When the rainy season arrived, the grasses and other plants grew tall and strong. The tree made new leaves that were green and glossy.

RAIN, GLORIOUS RAIN ...

Without plants, animals could not live in the savanna. Grasses, shrubs, and trees make shady places where animals can shelter from the hot sun. But that isn't all—the plants also provide the animals with food.

9

The tree was full of insects busily feeding on it. Sugary sap from the green shoots was food for all kinds of bugs and ants, and crawling caterpillars munched on the leaves.

YUM, JUICY LEAVES FOR LUNCH.

All sorts of animals eat plants, from insects to elephants. Plant food gives the animals energy and the minerals their bodies need to be healthy. Plant-eating animals are called herbivores.

A large caterpillar worked its way toward a clump of juicy leaves at the end of a twig. It did not notice the brightly colored bird sitting on a branch above it.

YUM! JUICY CATERPILLAR FOR LUNCH!

The bird bent its head to look at the caterpillar. In spite of its hairy spikes and orangey-red stripes, the bird knew it was good to eat.

In a flash, the bird reached down and grabbed the caterpillar in its beak. It flicked back its head and swallowed the caterpillar whole.

DOWN IN ONE!

Animals that eat other animals are known as carnivores. As well as energy, carnivores also get minerals from the food they eat. Some animals (including many humans) eat both plants and other animals—they are called omnivores.

Then the bird shook out its wings and settled back on the branch to wait for another meal to come along.

Every living thing, whether it is a plant or an animal, is food for something else.

Most animals only eat certain types of food.

The caterpillar that eats the leaves on the tree will not eat fruit or seeds, even though they grow on the same tree.

The bird that eats the caterpillar might also eat other insects, or even small lizards, but it will not eat leaves.

Animals and plants are linked together by the food that they eat. Scientists call this a food chain. Each link of the chain is food for the next link.

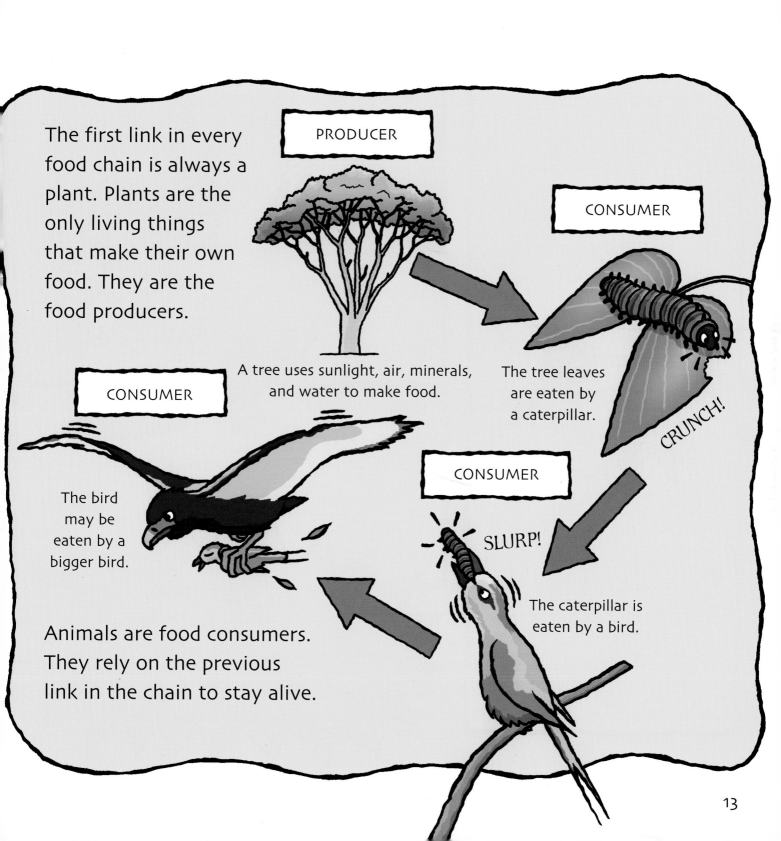

The first link in every food chain is always a plant. Plants are the only living things that make their own food. They are the food producers.

PRODUCER

CONSUMER

A tree uses sunlight, air, minerals, and water to make food.

The tree leaves are eaten by a caterpillar.

CRUNCH!

CONSUMER

CONSUMER

The bird may be eaten by a bigger bird.

SLURP!

The caterpillar is eaten by a bird.

Animals are food consumers. They rely on the previous link in the chain to stay alive.

13

As the afternoon wore on, it grew a little cooler and more animals came out to feed. The bird spread its wings and took to the air. A shadow fell on it from above. The shadow was made by an eagle.

EEEK!

With a loud shriek, the bird just managed to escape the eagle's outstretched claws. The bird darted away, its wings flapping wildly.

Disappointed, the eagle glided on. Below it, a small herd of zebra wandered across the grassland.

Animals that hunt and kill other animals are called predators, and the animals they hunt are known as prey.

As the zebras moved, their striped coats made it hard to separate one animal from another. One zebra was limping, and the rest of the herd traveled slowly so that it was not left behind.

ALL CLEAR!

Some people think a zebra's stripes help protect it from predators. When zebras bunch together in a group, their stripes overlap and the outline of each animal is harder to see. This makes it difficult for a predator to pick out any one animal.

The zebras stopped and lowered their heads to the grass. All except one. That zebra was on lookout. It kept its head up and swiveled its ears in all directions, checking for predators. But it did not see the lions hidden in the long grass.

15

The lionesses (female lions) had spotted the limping zebra. Keeping their bodies low to the ground, the lionesses slowly spread out around the herd.

TIME FOR SUPPER.

The lionesses knew they had one chance to catch their prey. They had to get as close to the herd as possible before any of the zebras noticed them.

SNORT!

Suddenly, another zebra raised its head and snorted nervously. In an instant, one of the big cats leapt forward, and the herd bolted in alarm.

Lions can run fast, but only for very short distances. If they don't catch their prey quickly, it will usually be able to outrun them.

For a moment, the limping zebra was lost in the blur of zig-zagging stripes. But it could not run as fast as the others.

All the lionesses joined the chase. They drove the unlucky zebra away from the herd. One lioness jumped at the zebra's neck and another at its back, and they dragged it down. Within moments, the zebra was dead.

WAIT FOR ME!

The two male lions in the group came forward, and the lionesses dropped back to let them feed first. Then the females ate. The cubs were allowed to feed last.

A group of lions is called a pride. There are always many more females than males in a pride. The females usually do the hunting. The males protect the pride from other lions.

WHEN IS IT OUR TURN?

MUNCH!

SCRUNCH!

While the lions feasted, a flock of large brown birds began to gather. They were vultures— part of the savanna's clean-up crew.

18

The vultures waited impatiently for the lions to finish. When all the lions had eaten their fill, they padded away to find a place to rest. They would not need to hunt again until tomorrow.

At once, the birds rushed in. Pushing and squabbling, they fought each other to get at the lions' leftovers.

More vultures landed, but the noise and movement brought other visitors, too. A couple of hyenas came to see what the vultures had found, and they wanted a share.

Snarling and snapping, the hyenas chased the vultures away. Then they settled down to finish off what was left of the zebra. They crunched up the bones and even the hooves with their strong jaws. Soon, there was little left but scraps of skin and bone.

Vultures and hyenas are both scavengers, although hyenas often hunt for their food as well. Scavengers eat what is left of another animal's kill. They also eat the bodies of animals that have died naturally of sickness or old age. In this way, no food is wasted.

The hyenas trotted off to search for something else to eat. The patch of grassland was quiet again—but it was not as empty as it seemed.

Thousands of insects scurried about in the grass. Some fed on the zebra scraps. Others laid eggs on them. When the eggs hatched, the scraps would provide food for the grubs.

COME ON EVERYBODY, DIVE IN!

As the days passed, the remaining bits of the zebra's body softened and rotted into the soil. Soon there was nothing left to show that the zebra had ever been there. But even these rotted bits had one last purpose.

In the soil, invisibly small living things called bacteria were hard at work. Bacteria break up dead animal and plant material into minerals and other chemicals.

MMMM! THIS WATER IS GOOD.

The last bits of the zebra's body were finally used up. The next time it rained, water soaked into the soil and the minerals dissolved in the water.

Plant roots sucked up the mineral-rich water and made healthy new stems, leaves, seeds, and fruit.

The plants were ready to start more food chains.

All living things produce waste material, such as dead leaves or dung. When plants and animals die, their bodies become waste material, too. All this waste material is broken down by other living things and used as food. As the waste is broken down, important chemicals are released into the air and soil. These chemicals are used by plants to help them grow. Then the plants are eaten by animals and the whole process starts again.

HOME,
SWEET
HOME!

THERE'S NO PLACE LIKE HOME

The place where an animal or a plant lives and grows best is called its habitat. The habitat gives the plant or animal the right amount of light, food, warmth, shelter, and a place where it can reproduce. A habitat can be big, like a savanna, or small, like a pond.

Most living things can only survive in the right kind of habitat. A plant that grows in the hot savanna cannot live on a cold mountain. A caterpillar that lives in a tree cannot live in a pond.

CAUGHT IN A WEB

Many habitats are shared by lots of different plants and animals. Some of these plants and animals belong to more than one food chain.

The leaves that feed a caterpillar, for example, may also be eaten by a giraffe. The eagle that missed the bird will happily eat a lizard instead. Lions eat antelopes and giraffes, as well as zebras.

When food chains are linked together, they make a food web.

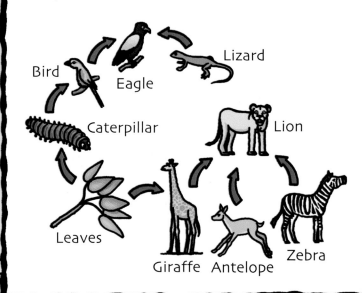

Bird

Eagle

Lizard

Caterpillar

Lion

Leaves

Giraffe Antelope

Zebra

POISONED LINKS

If something happens to one part of a food chain, it can affect all the other links in the chain.

For example, people sometimes spray plants with chemicals called pesticides. The pesticides kill the insects that feed on the plants. But other animals may eat the sprayed plants, too, or the insects that feed on them. The poison in the pesticides is passed on from animal to animal. If it does not kill an animal right away, it can build up in its body. If a predator eats enough poisoned prey, it will eventually die. Many eagles and other birds have died in this way.

TOP CAT

If plants are at one end of a food chain, a top predator is at the other end. Top predators are too powerful to be hunted by other animals as food. Instead, they die of illness or old age and their bodies are eaten by scavengers. Top predators are often fierce carnivores, such as lions and tigers. However, the most powerful top predators of all are not wild animals—they're humans!

I'M KING OF THE FOOD CHAIN ... I THINK!

25

TRY IT AND SEE

GROWING POWER

Most green plants start life as seeds. A seed contains almost everything it needs to make a new plant, but the new plant will only grow when it has the right conditions.

Try this experiment to find out what seeds and plants need to grow.

You will need:
- A bowl of clean water
- A teaspoon
- Seeds (mustard and cress, or sprouting seeds, such as alfalfa or lentils)
- Four clean, empty yogurt cups
- Cotton balls
- Water
- A shoebox

1 Put a teaspoon of seeds into the bowl of water and leave them to soak overnight. (You can skip this step if you are using mustard and cress.)

2 Number the yogurt cups 1, 2, 3, and 4. Put a thick layer of cotton balls into each yogurt cup. Sprinkle the cotton balls with water until damp.

3

Scatter a few seeds on top of the damp cotton balls in each cup. Put the cups somewhere warm and light.

4

Check the cups each day. Make sure the cotton balls stay moist. After a few days, you should see little white shoots and roots coming from your seeds. Keep watering them until you see lots of green leaves appearing on the shoots. This should take about seven days.

5

Your seeds have grown into small plants. Now let's see what happens to them when you change their conditions for growth.

Leave Cup 1 where it is, and go on watering it each day.

Leave Cup 2 where it is, but don't give the plants any more water.

Put Cup 3 inside the shoebox, and put the lid on the box. Water the plants as before, but keep the lid on the box so that they get no light.

Fill Cup 4 to the brim with water, and put plastic wrap over the top so that the plants get no air.

How different are the plants in your cups after another seven days?

CONSUMING FACTS

SPLAT!

There are a few plants that eat animals. They are called carnivorous plants. They mainly eat insects. One of the best-known is the Venus flytrap. When a fly lands on its hinged leaf, the leaf snaps shut, trapping the fly. The plant then dissolves the fly and absorbs the nutrients in it.

Lots of animals like to eat the large caterpillars that live on the mopane tree in the African savanna—and people do, too. Called mopane worms, the caterpillars are a favorite snack food of the people who live in the savanna. They are eaten fried, dried, or stewed in a sauce.

OH NO, NOT ANOTHER ONE!

Hunting is difficult work, and lions often go hungry. A lion needs to eat about 18 pounds (almost 8 kilograms) of meat a day—that's as much as a large turkey. But if it gets the chance it can eat six times as much as this.

GLOSSARY

carnivore—a meat-eating animal

consumer—animals that rely on the previous link in the food chain to stay alive

herbivores—plant-eating animals

photosynthesis—a process plants use to make food and oxygen

predators—animals that hunt and kill other animals

prey—an animal that is hunted by another animal

producer—plants that make their own food

savanna—flat, grassy plain that has only a few trees

ON THE WEB

FactHound offers a safe, fun way to find Internet sites related to this book. All of the sites on FactHound have been researched by our staff.

1. Visit *www.facthound.com*

2. Type in this special code for age-appropriate sites: 1404815953

3. Click on the FETCH IT button.

   Your trusty FactHound will fetch the best sites for you!

INDEX

Look for all of the books in the Science Works series:

A Drop in the Ocean:
The Story of Water
1-4048-0566-4

Charged Up:
The Story of Electricity
1-4048-0568-0

Cracking Up:
A Story About Erosion
1-4048-1594-5

Monster Bones:
The Story of a Dinosaur Fossil
1-4048-0565-6

The Rock Factory:
A Story of Rocks and Stones
1-4048-1596-1

Staying Alive:
The Story of a Food Chain
1-4048-1595-3

Sun Up, Sun Down:
The Story of Day and Night
1-4048-0567-2

Up, Down, All Around :
A Story of Gravity
1-4048-1597-X

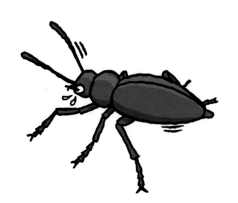